Digging into Financial Advice

Finding the Best Help for You to Invest

Will Taylor

WESTBOW
PRESS®
A DIVISION OF THOMAS NELSON
& ZONDERVAN

Copyright © 2020 Will Taylor.

All rights reserved. No part of this book may be used or reproduced by any means, graphic, electronic, or mechanical, including photocopying, recording, taping or by any information storage retrieval system without the written permission of the author except in the case of brief quotations embodied in critical articles and reviews.

This book is a work of non-fiction. Unless otherwise noted, the author and the publisher make no explicit guarantees as to the accuracy of the information contained in this book and in some cases, names of people and places have been altered to protect their privacy.

WestBow Press books may be ordered through booksellers or by contacting:

WestBow Press
A Division of Thomas Nelson & Zondervan
1663 Liberty Drive
Bloomington, IN 47403
www.westbowpress.com
1 (866) 928-1240

Because of the dynamic nature of the Internet, any web addresses or links contained in this book may have changed since publication and may no longer be valid. The views expressed in this work are solely those of the author and do not necessarily reflect the views of the publisher, and the publisher hereby disclaims any responsibility for them.

Any people depicted in stock imagery provided by Getty Images are models, and such images are being used for illustrative purposes only.
Certain stock imagery © Getty Images.

Scripture quotations are from the ESV® Bible (The Holy Bible, English Standard Version®), copyright © 2001 by Crossway, a publishing ministry of Good News Publishers. Used by permission. All rights reserved.

ISBN: 978-1-9736-8467-1 (sc)
ISBN: 978-1-9736-8469-5 (hc)
ISBN: 978-1-9736-8468-8 (e)

Library of Congress Control Number: 2020901700

Print information available on the last page.

WestBow Press rev. date: 02/10/2020

Table of Contents

Foreword vii
Chapter 1   There Is Money to Be
            Made Giving Financial Advice 1
Chapter 2   The Sales Pitch: From
            Business TV and Across the Desk 7
Chapter 3   The Keys to Financial
            Success and Knowledge:
            Common Stock and the
            Financial Plan 13
Chapter 4   How Do These People Get
            Paid Anyway? 21
Chapter 5   What About Dividends
            and Sporadic Investors? 29
Chapter 6   Why Do I Buy High and Sell Low? ... 35
Chapter 7   Asset Allocation and Robo Investing .. 45
Chapter 8   Discount Brokers—the
            Big Dog on the Block 53

Chapter 9   Traditional Brokerage
with Mutual Funds 65
Chapter 10 The Flexibility of No-Load
Mutual Funds 75
Chapter 11 RIAs and Bank Wealth
Management, a.k.a. Trust
Departments: Fiduciary
Services Providers 79
Chapter 12 Other Types of
Investments to Consider 85
Chapter 13 Alternative Investments 91
Chapter 14 Back to the Heart of It:
The Financial Plan 95
Chapter 15 Real Risk Tolerance and
the Need to Save More 99

About the Author 103

Foreword

In clear and direct style, Mr. Taylor helps us navigate through the maze of brokers, banks, insurance agents, and other financial service providers selling stocks, bonds, mutual funds, annuities, ETFs, CDs, commodities and alternative investments. Each chapter is "bite-sized" while being heavily infused with the wisdom of experience to candidly help you understand advantages and pitfalls of various categories of investments and motivations of investment providers. We emerge from the maze having unearthed many buried treasures of investment knowledge and with a new recognition that a personal financial plan supporting our own goals, based on our own situation is a vital and achievable compass for our financial journey through life. Insightful reading for young adults to senior citizens, modest wage-earners and wealthy.

Tom Richard

Chapter 1

There Is Money to Be Made Giving Financial Advice

Why should a fool have money in his hand to buy wisdom when he has no sense?
—Proverbs 17:16 ESV

This stock will rise 100 percent in one year! Check out this website. The analyst who bought Amazon at $100 per share has predicted the last five stock market rallies and corrections! Penny stocks is where the real money is; invest with us! Now is the time to invest in these mutual funds that will carefully and successfully lead you to a long and worry-free retirement! Want to only grow as the market grows and avoid any loss? Talk to our experienced and caring representatives! If you want to learn about the easiest way to retirement, come have dinner on us and learn the secret of a secure retirement!

Financial advice for the average investor is everywhere. High quality, competent, and accurate financial advice may be not so abundant. As this is being written, the stock markets appear to be on an endless rally with many new records being set. It is a time of robust joy as stock portfolios rise to new levels with almost no effort. There is very little concern about the quality or accuracy of information coming from the experts, as virtually all investments with any level of stocks are going up at unbelievable speed.

The current market conditions will not continue and may reverse in the time it takes to write this book on financial advice from the professionals. The rally will stop, and smiles will turn to frowns as gains disappear. It is the nature of the stock market; for evidence one only needs to look at history.

There is money to be made in the investment of publicly traded equities, but many do not understand the nature of the investment. Those who do seek help to invest often are subjected to poor and expensive advice that helps the salesperson more than the investor. The salesperson has little risk and can be more of a detriment than help to the investor who is taking the risk. We are going to look at the providers of financial advice to the average person and examine their motives and methods.

In today's world of electronic trading and record keeping, there are many methods to trade and own stock. Stock is a term that is the same for our purposes as equities and is defined by Investopedia as: "A stock is a type of security that signifies ownership in a corporation and represents a claim on part of the corporation's assets and earnings." The shareholder's value in a company rises and falls as the stock price changes. If the company is doing well, then the stock price usually rises, and the shareholders' value of their investment rises. On the downside, when a company is not doing well, the stock price usually falls, and the stockholder's value of the investment falls.

The best of all worlds would be if a stock price only goes up. This, of course, is not possible but at times some stocks seem to be on an endless rise. Stock values that have risen from a single digit price per share to values in the hundreds or thousands can ignite a desire to own stock. The huge potential gain sometimes leads inexperienced investors to believe that a hot tip on a stock to buy will lead to an inside track and guaranteed wealth.

The key is to know which stock prices are going to rise and which ones are going to fall. If that knowledge was known, then the investor could invest only in the stocks that are rising, sell the stock at the maximum price before the price declines, and then invest in another stock that is rising. It is easy to see the desired result. Paying for knowledge that would tell the investor when to buy and sell would have immense value if the advice is correct and the price of the advice does not overshadow the gain from using the advice.

This is where the use of financial advice must be carefully considered. There are many methods to invest in stocks, but each has positives and negatives. Each service provider has resources for information and sources for current recommendations. While there are many jokes regarding the quality of data and value of adviser information, an adviser who genuinely cares for clients and provides realistic recommendations based on the client's needs and goals can be quite beneficial to the client's success. Conversely, advisers who care more about gaining additional assets to manage rather than provide quality care will do more harm than good.

Each investor has needs and concerns that can affect the specific makeup of his or her stock portfolio. Different reasons to invest include the need for income and/or asset growth, the need to have more or less risk and to use various types of equity investments such as individual stocks, mutual funds, and exchange traded funds (ETFs). This wide diversity of stocks, investors, and types of advice is what makes investing in stocks such a strange variation of players and opinions. We are going to examine the various players in the world of the stock market. It will not be an all-inclusive list but will list the primary players who the average investor would encounter.

Chapter 2

The Sales Pitch: From Business TV and Across the Desk

He who loves money will not be satisfied with money, nor he who loves wealth with his income; this also is vanity.
—*Ecclesiastes 5:10 ESV*

Have you ever watched TV stations that focus on the business of investments? Three that come to mind are Fox Business, CNBC, and Bloomberg. These stations and others like them provide their viewers with ever-changing news on the stock market in general or a specific part of the market such as the oil industry. An "expert" is brought in at times, usually an analyst from a prestigious brokerage firm or investment company to provide insight. At some point in the discussion, the host will usually ask the guest, "What are you buying now," and "Would you be a buyer of the company being discussed?" The guest then gives a short list of investments, usually stocks, considered in his or her opinion, a good investment.

This is an interesting game being played on TV. It is somewhat fast paced, and topics change frequently. The TV host must balance the desire to provide helpful and relevant information with the need to increase ratings and draw advertising dollars. The show's producers know that viewers want to know information on the stock market especially and other financial news in general; the guest wants to gain clients, prestige, and wealth through the visibility of the TV spot. The greater the accuracy and timeliness of the information being provided, the greater the profitability to all.

Unlike advice given on television, when a prospective client seeks information from a financial services provider, the provider has a brief window of opportunity to convince a prospect of the value of the services. In a typical situation the investor meets with a financial adviser, principal, or other important sounding name to see if the expert can provide insight and help to the investor. The adviser being interviewed wants to appear as a problem solver, enlightener, and adept on the financial markets and investing. The adviser also has to convince the investor of his/her greater ability than the investor would do on his or her own, under the care of the expert down the street, or at a different website.

Motive for these meetings is usually to build wealth for all concerned in these conversations. These experts are providing information, much of it having to do with economics and historical performance of investments on a national and international perspective. National and international economics can influence the financial markets and investments being suggested to the investor. The numbers, charts, graphs, and information can be overwhelming. A specific direction of the conversation is usually orchestrated by the presenter to convince the investor that the service being offered is exactly what the investor needs to be successful at investing.

In some situations, the representative giving the

information will have many experts in support. The presentation has been researched and tried and statistics determined so the presenter knows what information is received favorably and what may be misunderstood or taken negatively in the path to gain the investor as a client. At its base, it is a well-rehearsed sales pitch.

It is not all negative for the investor. Most experts will ask very relevant questions such as the plans for this money, the overall goals, and the level of experience with investments. Questions like these do need to be answered to provide the best service to the investor. However, most of the presentation has very little to do with helping the client but more about a sales proposition to convince the prospective investor of the expert's unique ability to manage money for each individual prospect.

Each prospect needs to develop ears to hear where the discussion turns from information gathering to sales pitch. There are many examples on the internet and in business print listing steps and relevant questions to find a financial adviser. The items in these articles are very good to know when considering a financial adviser or website for investments. The most informative are those articles not published by service providers to guard against a list that conveniently outlines all the attributes of the publisher.

Chapter 3

The Keys to Financial Success and Knowledge: Common Stock and the Financial Plan

Without counsel plans fail, but with many advisers they succeed.
—Proverbs 15:22 ESV

So then why do we invest in stocks, bonds, mutual funds, exchange traded funds, and other similar investments that are available in today's fast-paced world? We could invest in commercial or rental real estate, gold, silver, farmland, commodities, futures, options, bitcoin, or numerous other investments, but why are stocks such a widely used investment to grow wealth? The easy answer is the long and profitable success of stocks to create wealth, which, of course, then allows the investor to accomplish his/her goals.

Obvious needs for wealth are to fund retirement, buy a house, purchase a new car, or just save for a rainy day—whatever that implies. Our lives can be very complicated with many things going on at any time. Since having wealth helps make these complicated things somewhat easier, building abundance is the goal. These goals are very personal, since each investor is different, and justifies a detailed analysis to address each goal in the most efficient way possible.

Each investor needs a financial plan to meet these goals head on and provide the best solution. The term "financial plan" has very different meanings and levels of complexity. As each type of investment provider is discussed in the following pages, the various levels of a financial plan will also be summarized.

According to Investopedia, a financial plan is "a comprehensive statement of an individual's long-term objectives for security and well-being and a detailed savings and investing strategy for achieving those objectives. A financial plan may be created independently or with the help of a financial planner specifically trained and following specific procedures and ethical standards.

The plan should contain analysis on calculating net worth, determining cash flow, determining retirement needs and steps to reach the lifestyle anticipated, review and summary of current and needed insurance coverage, asset allocation best suited for the long term, tax calculation and strategies to avoid and reduce tax liability, and an estate plan that would include the necessary estate documents to provide protection and to benefit heirs."

In many respects the financial plan is more important—more necessary—and should be discussed to a greater degree than any hot tip or successful investment program. The plan will outline where the initial focus should be based on the goals and current situation of the client and outline a process of subsequent steps. Since each of us has very different lives, the more individualized the plan is able to be, the greater benefit to the client.

The investments should follow the finding in the plan and be subjected to the plan. In most investment presentations, the investments and the level of skill of the expert are touted much more than the financial plan. The focus on the expert and the investments is sort of like: shoot, ready, aim. The outcome will result in something, but it may not at all be what is wanted or in the best interest of the investor.

Our culture does not like financial planning. It goes against our standard operating procedure of appearing to be self-reliant and financially brilliant. In other words, to appear as something that most of us are not. Our culture demands that we do not show weakness or appear to be less than successful and always happy and in control.

My experience as a financial planner was at times frustrating. I had seen the benefit of financial planning through my training and by completing a plan for my wife and me. I wanted to help others with the power available in a comprehensive plan. I could also see how providing a financial plan could turn into a long-lasting client relationship. What I found was that very few people were interested in having a financial plan done. The company I worked for touted the plan as being so very helpful and even offered the plan at no cost or given as a prize of a drawing. Even then no one wanted to go through the process.

Perhaps the reasoning was "no news is good news," or perhaps they have convinced themselves that it was all under control, and no help was needed. I think some saw my profession as one to distrust, and so there was no need to even talk to any of us. From the financial plans I was able to do for others, it was clear there was a real need for the service, as very few of us have it all together. I also believe the offer for financial planning is often declined because so many realize they need help but do not want anyone else to know it.

Look at the number of car loans that extend further than the average period of car ownership. Consider the number of cars that are leased rather than purchased so the owner can have a more expensive car than the person's actual cash flow will allow. Car and truck commercials do not usually focus on the retail price to entice a purchase, but the lease payment or expected monthly payment is shown with emphasis. There are situations where a lease or long-term payment makes sense, but usually the payment is a burden to an already stretched cash flow.

Another point to consider is the amount of credit card debt that is held by those who have not experienced any financial emergency (not yet anyway) but simply do not want to wait until they have the cash to buy items that will provide the appearance of wealth. A sizable number of households have used credit cards in excess and are one missed paycheck from financial disaster.

A financial plan with a focus on cash flow and debt reduction might be very sobering but very helpful if a return to solvency is the goal. Many households at the edge of financial disaster erroneously see the big rallies and growth potential of stocks as a way out. A comprehensive financial plan provided by a caring and competent financial planner looking out for the client's interest is the best remedy.

It seems that our culture's motto was illustrated by Robert Quillen. His thoughts on the American culture are that we Americans spend money we do not have on things we do not need to impress people we do not like. An in-depth financial plan will dig into all these items that have accumulated for the wrong reasons. The financial plan may reveal much deeper problems than needing a method to invest in stocks, as the client may be in serious financial trouble. Financial guidance for investing must at times be placed on hold to work on debt reduction and cash management.

The choice of the financial planner is important. Many financial professionals advertise themselves as financial planners. Unfortunately, most of these financial planners use financial planning as a tool to find clients and increase the asset level they manage, thereby increasing their fee income. There are professional organizations that have strict ethical standards to be followed, but at times these standards are discarded in the search for new clients.

Since financial planning can be extremely personal in that it takes in all aspects of one's financial life, the process of the plan and the ethics involved with gathering and using the data needs to be considered when choosing a financial planner. It is easy to imagine that if one's entire personal financial picture is laid out, the wrong person could easily take advantage of the situation and use the data for personal gain rather than for the benefit of the person providing the data.

Most of us are very guarded with who and how much we share our financial information and history. Consider our attitude regarding sharing information with the IRS. While most us are honest taxpayers, we still do not even want to share any of our financial information with the IRS. There is simply not a level of trust in this entity. Okay, using the IRS as the more trusted entity may be a poor example, but the thought is still usable. Our financial data is very personal to us. We are also hesitant to share with an individual we may have just been introduced to or a financial expert who is a friend or a friend of a friend.

A level of trust and confidence needs to be developed or gained before many would-be investors share their financial information. We want to be sure if information is shared that it is kept confidential and used only for our ultimate benefit to make our situation better. A standard of care and concern is needed by the service provider that places the client's interest above the interests of the service provider.

Chapter 4

How Do These People Get Paid Anyway?

◆──────◆──────◆

Whoever is greedy for unjust gain troubles his own household, but he who hates bribes will live.

—*Proverbs 15:27 ESV*

There are organizations that practice this duty to provide a high standard of care to the client and the client's information. The highest level of care is to be a fiduciary. The term fiduciary has been tossed around quite a bit in the last few years as the government has taken steps to create a level of care for money managers. There have been many attempts and provisions put forth to provide this high level of care, but as government changes, so does the focus.

To be a fiduciary is to provide a level of care that places the client's needs and best interest above all needs and concerns of the individual or firm providing the service. This level of care is extraordinary and somewhat rare in the financial management world due primarily to the method that most financial adviser firms are compensated. Consider your own actions in the following situations:

Scenario one: you are providing a service to someone, and your personal income is based on the items and amount you sell. In your product line you have the following items for sale for the client. Item A costs the client $1,000, item B costs $750, and item C costs $250. If the overall purpose of the items you are selling is simply different ways to accomplish the same thing, which item would you be more likely try to sell with greater enthusiasm? In other words, if the person you are selling to has no real concept of the typical cost, which item would you be more likely to sell?

Financial advisers and their organizations can provide an investment that has the same focus and composition but has different level of fees taken, depending on the arrangement between the client and the adviser. The result is that many different clients will have the same investment but varying results because of the difference in the level of fees taken.

Scenario two: you are providing a service to someone, and your personal income is not based on specific items you sell; your bonus and job security are largely based on the number of clients you have and the value of financial investment that your clients have with you. This means that unless you maintain a high number of accounts with an ever-growing account balance, your bonus may suffer, and your job may be in question. You must continue to provide services to a growing balance of assets.

Many wealth management services owned by community and commercial banks use this method to pay their officers. There is pressure to continually build the asset size under management. This encourages the officer to continually ask current clients if there are more assets that can be transferred and continually work to find new clients. There is also the potential that the officers will place their clients in more aggressive portfolios than is in the client's best interest.

Scenario three: you are providing a service to a

client and the fee is based on the value of the account balance. The fee is a set percentage of the account value, and your personal income is a percentage of the overall fee. The remaining portion of the fee goes to the company you are affiliated with to pay for overhead, technology, and back office help. So as the account value increases, so does the income you receive. If the account value falls, then your income will decrease.

Scenario four: you are providing a service to someone, and your personal income and personal bonus are not based on the specific items you sell. Your job security is based on the profitability of the company overall and your personal actions in working to meet the expectations of the company.

In reviewing these scenarios, all can be used in providing a fiduciary duty to their clients and all can be lacking in the carrying out consistent levels of being a fiduciary. The primary item of measurement is the financial gain or risk that the service provider carries. It comes back to money and the ethical standards of the provider. These methods of compensation or combination of them are used extensively in the financial services industry.

It may be difficult to maintain a consistent level of impartiality and placing the client's interest above all else if you are working under the first three examples just shared. The tendency to use the product with the higher fee to you or the need to hold on to client's assets through means of advice shared must be a temptation at times. Financial advisers face these challenges, and those seeking financial services need to be aware of possible alternatives.

As the different types of service providers in the financial services industry are examined, the filters used will be in terms of compensation, degree of financial planning, level of addressing the fiduciary standard to provide the highest level of care to the clients, and other characteristics that are used in these various providers. The methods of providing financial advice vary widely as do the individuals who provide this service inside each method. As each type of service provider is examined, it is with a broad brush since there are so many variations within each example.

Providing financial advice is a very competitive business, and there are many casualties in the form of job losses and business failures each year. There is the potential for a very profitable lifestyle for those who can gather the most assets for an extended period. Business growth also occurs as firms buy others and achieve economies of scale.

Reputation is paramount in the business and word of mouth referrals from one client to a prospect is a primary method of growth. Only the older readers will remember the slogan "when E. F. Hutton speaks, people listen." This was a slogan that was well received on TV and radio in the 1970s. Two individuals are discussing investments in a noisy environment such as a restaurant, coffee shop, or airplane with many different conversations going on at the same time. However whenever one individual says, "My broker is E. F Hutton, and E. F. Hutton says …" the surrounding conversations immediately stop and all in the area lean in to hear what E. F. Hutton has to say. It was a very popular ad for the firm.

The E. F. Hutton firm has long since been swallowed by a competitor, which is the way of many firms. In hindsight, if the advice was so desirable, why didn't all the folks who drop their own conversations to listen to the advice of the oracle known as E. F. Hutton have an account with E. F. Hutton themselves? It is one of the many points of the financial advice industry that played well to the masses. The ad caused the listener to think that this firm knows what it is doing. It is helping people, and the advice is correct. It was a great draw to ask more about the services the company provides.

Being perceived as a place where questions are answered and where clients have been helped is very desirable for an investment firm. We want to be treated at least fairly and honestly, but more likely we want to be treated like we are special. We want to think the service provider sees us as worthy of extra attention and perhaps inside information, if it is not illegal, of course. We want our pride to be stroked.

Chapter 5

What About Dividends and Sporadic Investors?

❖

For the love of money is a root of all kinds of evils. It is through this craving that some have wandered away from the faith and pierced themselves with many pangs.
—*1 Timothy 6:10 ESV*

The typical equity investor wants the investment to never decrease in value and to grow faster than the rate of inflation and of course faster than their friends' and bothersome relatives' portfolio. No one wants to admit his or her portfolio did worse than anticipated or in discussion find out the portfolio was at the bottom when compared to others. A lower return implies poor judgment, a lack of understanding and bad decisions. This may or not be true, but again our pride rises, and usually genuine bad decisions follow.

It is of no value to compare portfolios to others because of the varying asset allocation. According to Investopedia, "asset allocation is an investment strategy that aims to balance risk and reward by apportioning a portfolio's assets according to an individual's goals, risk tolerance, and investment horizon. The three main asset classes - equities, fixed-income, and cash and equivalents - have different levels of risk and return, so each will behave differently over time."

As the percentage of the three main asset classes vary, the return to the portfolio will substantially change. Since the return is closely correlated to the asset allocation of the portfolio, it is not logical to compare the returns of portfolios that have different asset allocations. It is like comparing apples and oranges. The accomplishment of the goals in the financial plan in relation to the expected progress is a more helpful measure.

Since we are talking about stocks as the primary tool of asset growth, we need to understand how this is accomplished. Stocks increase asset value by the appreciation of the stock price and, with many stocks, the receipt of a dividend. Whether a stock pays a dividend is dependent on the company's overall philosophy and goals. For example, Apple Computer pays a dividend, Amazon does not. Both are very successful companies that are currently some of the most widely traded stocks in the market. Both companies have seen strong growth in the stock price.

The level of dividend also varies with the company. Utility companies traditionally have a higher dividend yield, which is the annual dividend received in dollars divided by current stock price, compared to companies considered to be growth stocks. Since utility stock prices do not usually vary much, they pay a strong dividend to entice investment.

Amazon is an example of a rapidly growing company. The stock price is rising as company earnings and demand for Amazon's services increases. The payment of a dividend is not currently needed to entice investment. Also, companies not paying dividends can keep the cash in reserve to grow through product and service enhancements, acquisition, or for other purposes.

A very basic analogy of the benefit received with a dividend is with rental real estate. An investor purchases a house or apartment building for basically two purposes: to receive rental income and to achieve appreciation in the value of the real estate over time. There is also a tax advantage to some investors based on purchase of real estate, but this illustration will be limited to income and asset growth, which can be seen with many stocks as well.

The dividend income from the stock would be analogous to the rent payment, and the growth of the value of the stock purchased can be aligned with the increase in value from real estate. If income is the primary reason for holding stock, then a consideration of the yield from the stock would be important when making a purchase. If growth of the stock is more important than receiving a steady stream of income, then stocks with a lower yield or perhaps with no dividend at all may be more suitable.

There is another valuable point of comparison with rental real estate and stocks. Owners of real estate do not buy and sell as frequently as many stock owners. It is more complicated to trade real estate in comparison to stocks, but perhaps stock owners should think about the advantages of infrequent buying and selling of real estate. Conversely, there are equity investments in the form of real estate investment trusts, (REITS), mutual funds, and ETFs that specialize in real estate ownership. These equity securities with a base in real estate usually provide a fairly high level of dividend as the rental income is partially distributed to the asset owner.

Chapter 6

Why Do I Buy High and Sell Low?

❖

As soon as they saw it, they were astounded; they were in panic; they took to flight.
—*Psalm 48:5 ESV*

Both stock and real estate are considered long-term investments due to their nature and level of risk. However, stock markets are much more volatile due to the ease of trading, which can cause an emotional reaction to buy and sell impulsively. When this happens over a period of years, the advice of the ages to buy at a lower price and sell at a higher price is usually reversed and investors buy high and sell low.

This is where experience and/or heeding the advice

of a seasoned financial adviser with the client's best interest in mind can be extremely valuable. Advice on the nature of the market and the characteristics of stock—that being a long-term investment—is given frequently but is not heeded by the stockholder.

Consider Neal, a sporadic stock investor. When the stock market is going down and the news is virtually all negative, Neal is very relieved at his good fortune to be watching the market move downward from the sidelines. Conversely, when the market is rising, Neal feels he is missing out. He wants to be in the market and looks for the opportunity and the perfect stock to take him to new fortunes.

Neal is hesitant as he remembers when the market falls and thinks that possibly the current rise is a temporary move and soon it will go down. He remembers how good it feels to have no stock investment when the market falls. That feeling can be more satisfying than the uncertainty of owning stock in a rising market since there is always the risk that the market will turn, and the profit he has gained will be lost.

The usual result is that Neal will buy into the

market just as it tops out and starts to consistently go down. His hesitancy in making the purchase creates the almost certain potential for failure. As the market turns, and Neal panics due to the apparent reversal of stock price, he sells. Neal likes the idea of the potential profit but has not grasped what it means to be a long-term investment. He, like many part-time investors, wants the profit without the downside risk. Unfortunately, this is not the nature of the investment.

Stock prices fluctuate and have risk; it is in their DNA. If stocks did not have risk, they would not have the potential return that they have. One never hears about non brokerage CD values falling, then rising, and then falling again; it is not in the nature of certificates of deposit to fluctuate in value. The interest that is paid on CDs can vary, but the initial investment in the CD will hardly ever be lost. Correspondingly, since there is very little risk with the CD, the return in relation to other investments is very low. It is a trade-off—the higher the risk the higher the potential return and vice versa.

The investor needs to learn the nature of risk in general and the nature of risk of stocks especially if investment is being considered. This is where the professional adviser can be of assistance. With any purchase, knowledge of the investment is paramount to match the investment with the needs of the investor. In the world of stock assets, many choices are available. The competency, cost, level of hands-on involvement, and add-on features of the financial expert will vary broadly as well.

Consider a possible investor, Sam, who comes into money unexpectedly due to a settlement for an injury. The amount is less than $500,000. Sam is in his fifties and has worked hard his whole life. He did not get any breaks and did whatever he had to do to get by and try to raise a family. This was more money than he could imagine, but he did the right thing by seeking out someone in wealth management.

Sam is seeing this money as the answer to many of his worries, and he has the common sense to know he does not know what to do. This world of investments and even savings is completely foreign to him to the point that he does not even know what questions to ask. He knows he will need to use at least the income that is generated with the investment and maybe part of the original settlement to pay off debts and help meet current and future expenses. What kind of answers will he receive for the questions he does ask from the various types of service providers? Will information for Sam's benefit be given even if he does not ask?

Consider another type of client. Jennifer is a successful businessperson who has spent her adult life working and making financial decisions. She has learned about stocks and many other investments from her education, through her work, coworkers, and the culture in which she lives. Assets are accumulating in retirement accounts, personal holdings, and some inheritance. This is what many would call a privileged individual. How will Jennifer be received in service centers for asset management in comparison to Sam in the previous paragraph?

Many providers will not take the time to work with Sam. He would be too much trouble and time consuming due to his complete inexperience and limited resources. Knowing that Sam will be taking distributions from the account on a regular basis implies he will not be the ideal client. While the settlement may be large in Sam's opinion, many providers have very high minimum levels of the amount of investable cash and overall net worth. These providers are only chasing the higher-income wealthy clients.

Unfortunately, some providers see Sam as the perfect client because of his ignorance. The provider will be able to recommend investments with high fees for the provider's benefit while still helping Sam. The provider will explain the investment being recommended, and it will be in terms that Sam will mostly understand. However, the overall picture will still be vague, and Sam will leave the provider with the thought, *I'm not exactly sure what I am invested in, but my provider sounds like he knows what he is talking about.* In other words, Sam is putting all his trust in the provider who he just met but has been convinced by the salesmanship that he is making the right decision.

Assuming Jennifer's assets that are in cash (checking, savings, money markets, certificates of deposit, etc.), mutual funds, stocks, bonds, ETFs, etc., are at least mid to high six figures, providers will be clambering for her business. Her assets would appear to be the result of a conscious long-term effort to grow her net worth and show that she is interested in keeping the assets invested and even consistently being added to in the foreseeable future. The provider can see a profitable client here and will dedicate substantial time and effort to gain Jennifer's business.

This effort will be primarily in the form of developing a relationship with Jennifer in which the provider convinces Jennifer of the provider's interest in her future growth of assets. Most of the sales pitch will include multiple charts and graphs of many colors on high-quality paper. The provider's name and logo will be strategically located in many places with the best possible contact information.

Jennifer will probably be offered a meal in a very nice or trendy restaurant to further discuss the qualifications of the provider and how likable and easy to talk to the provider is. Depending on Jennifer's level of assets in relation to the provider's target client, Jennifer may enjoy free tickets to a desired sporting event, concert, or other event that is of interest to Jennifer in order to make the sale. The provider focuses on impressing Jennifer and on building the relationship to help Jennifer see that the provider will be her best friend ever and provide access to prestige events at no cost.

Of course, there is a cost for this elaborate sales pitch. The prospective provider has determined the future fee income that Jennifer will provide to the firm in general and to the provider personally, and with the expectation that Jennifer will be a client for many years, the prospective provider will pull out the stops to spend money now to impress Jennifer for the future.

Whether to take Sam, Jennifer, or any client is very much in the provider's right to pick and choose their client base. Individuals needing financial help must be aware that as they seek help and are interviewing prospective providers, the individual is also being considered as being worthwhile or not. If a cool response is being felt from a prospective provider, it may be that the individual does not meet the requirements of the provider he or she is considering.

If it seems the provider is simply running through a sales pitch and not really personalizing the recommendation to align with the prospective client's entire financial picture, the provider may be more focused on his/her benefit than the prospective client's best interest. The individual should simply go elsewhere. Tickets to a ball game do not help a portfolio grow; a sound financial plan with limited fees is needed.

Chapter 7

Asset Allocation and Robo Investing

*When pride comes, then comes disgrace,
but with the humble is wisdom.*
—*Proverbs 11:2 ESV*

Some providers will accept any size of investment, but service levels usually vary with the amount of funds being invested. Please note the adverb "usually" in the previous sentence because there are exceptions to the rule. In today's world, these exceptions are worth considering because these may be the folks that really care about their clients' success no matter the account size.

As we look at the various providers, we will do so with a broad brush. There are exceptions to every scenario and platform of provider. Like so many service industries, technology plays a major role in providing the service and in varying levels of personal service. A personal touch by one specific professional with responsibility for a particular account list is still very prominent. The other extreme is a service that has virtually no personal contact unless initiated by the client. Any contact to the company will usually not be to a specific individual but to a phone number or chat line that will reach a bank of similarly trained individuals with an equal level of responsibility and training.

The newest and perhaps the fastest-growing service is the entirely online and tech-controlled system called robo investing. This system is very high tech and is the favorite of many younger investors. There is no human contact unless the investor really wants to talk to a representative. The account is opened online, of course. The investor chooses what asset allocation will be used for the investment.

Robo-investing firms take their fee as a percentage of the asset value. This percentage is usually at or less than 1 percent of the account value. The fee is calculated on an annual basis and is easily found in the information online with the application. The various firms will vary in the level of fees and specific investments offered, but the basics are that the client chooses a portfolio of ETFs or mutual funds that is a specific asset allocation.

The asset allocation that is appropriate to the investor is best determined through the process of financial planning. The robo-investing program usually does not have a very robust financial planning platform. There may be a part of the application that implies financial planning and will contain a series of drop-down boxes on the website that will place the investor in a category of financial condition. From these choices a summary is obtained, and projections on the growth and income expected will be available for review. This is not the type of financial plan that is needed to gain a knowledgeable picture of one's complete financial picture.

Asset allocation is extremely important in determining the long-term return of all investment accounts. The specific asset allocation may be as much as 90 to 95 percent of the return. In other words, of all the factors that can affect the return on a portfolio, virtually all of it is settled when the asset allocation is decided. This is an amazing consequence of a decision that is often passed over with a quick question or two while numerous conversations, PowerPoints, research papers, and sales pitches will be dedicated to the remaining 5 to 10 percent of potential return.

In determining the asset allocation, the level of risk is ascertained. As previously mentioned, the higher the level of risk, the higher the potential return. So then why not just choose the higher level of risk since the return will be the highest? An important detail is that the highest level of risk will provide the highest level of *potential* return. This does not guarantee the return; it is that the specific investments being used are believed to be able to provide the stated return over a long period of time. To obtain this expected level of return, the investment can go through many ups and downs over time.

Robo investing is primarily focused on the asset allocation. If the investor wants minimal cost and minimal involvement, the robo-investing service is an excellent way to go. The investor needs to understand what is going on and to be comfortable with the asset allocation chosen. Quite often investors with limited experience will see the trend like the current rising market and believe their investments will continue to perform as they most recently have, which is a serious error.

The various firms offering robo-investing have different options. Some of the companies are solely dedicated to high-tech low-touch process while others come from the high-touch investment service and are providing the robo-investing to capture some of the business of this growing trend. Within the high-touch providers providing robo services, there is the hope for future conversion of the robo clients to the high-touch services with higher fees at some time in the future. Hopefully as the account balance grows, the client will come to expect more services, and with the additional services come additional costs.

The investor needs to remain focused on the overwhelming contribution that asset allocation provides to the return. This point will be mentioned numerous times since this is where return is determined. Providers hope that the client will keep reaching out to change investments and thereby incur fees. Investors need to understand that at times the cost of additional changes is not providing additional return in an efficient manner. It is costing more in fees to provide limited additional return to a portfolio that may be running efficiently. Using robo-investing services with low fees is one way to provide this efficient return.

Exchange traded funds (ETFs) are the primary instrument used by robo investments. According to Bing, "an ETF is an investment fund traded on stock exchanges, much like stocks. An ETF holds assets such as stocks, commodities, or bonds, and trades close to its net asset value over the course of the trading day. Most ETFs track an index, such as a stock index or bond index." Like a mutual fund, there are fees in the investment that pay for the management for the investment. These fees are usually substantially lower than most mutual funds apart from many funds that providers of ETFs offer and index funds. It is highly competitive, and this competition is driving fees down to the advantage of the investor.

As the definition states, most ETFs are classified

as index ETFs. Investopedia defines an index as "An index is an indicator or measure of something, and in finance, it typically refers to a statistical measure of change in a securities market. In the case of financial markets, stock, and bond market indices consist of a hypothetical portfolio of securities representing a particular market or a segment of it. (You cannot invest directly in an index.) The S&P 500 and the US Aggregate Bond Index are common benchmarks for the American stock and bond markets, respectively." A stock or bond index is a method of substantiation or a reference to follow how a class of investment is doing. The most common stock indices are the Dow Jones Industrial Average and the Standard and Poor's (S&P) 500. These two indices are quoted most often in the media and provide a reference point for stock investors.

The S&P 500 stock index is a basket of five hundred stocks that Standard & Poor's has determined are the five hundred best representative of larger companies listed in the US stock exchanges. Individual stocks are classified into sectors such as health care, energy, utilities, technology, etc. The return of this index is widely used as a comparison of how stock portfolios, mutual funds, and individual stock have performed. An investment is considered a success if it can beat the S&P 500 on a consistent basis. It is not easy to do, and consistent success over the index is very rare. There are also indices to match up with small capitalization stocks, foreign stocks, bonds, treasury bonds, high yield bonds, etc. The list of indices is long.

Chapter 8

Discount Brokers—the Big Dog on the Block

◆━━━◆━━━◆

For the protection of wisdom is like the protection of money, and the advantage of knowledge is that wisdom preserves the life of him/her who has it.
—*Ecclesiastes 7:12 ESV*

Very sizable participants in the world of investments are the brokerage firms that offer more than robo investing. These companies provide a very wide range of investment services and serve clients from all levels of income and net worth in a vast array of services. Examples of this service are Charles Schwab, TD Ameritrade, Fidelity, and E*Trade. The most common service offered is discount brokerage. These companies advertise regularly on business and sports TV with a message of low brokerage costs and tools to help with investments. The client can call for investment assistance, and offices are available in many cities and smaller metropolitan areas.

Charles Schwab, TD Ameritrade, and Fidelity recently introduced free stock and ETF trading if the trade is completed online. This is the latest salvo in the battle for the investor. With no brokerage cost to complete a trade, new and very evident pressure is being placed on the higher-service, higher-cost brokers. An even more recent change is the purchase of TD Ameritrade by Charles Schwab. Schwab is becoming a massive provider of financial services.

As this new marketing plan of zero commissions is introduced, many have been asking, "What's the catch?" There really isn't one, as these companies are simply gathering assets that will be more profitable in the long run than competing in the lowest commissions battle for business. These companies make money on the cash that investors hold. The difference between the interest that is paid to account holders and the interest charged to investors who seek loans is profitable to the provider. Fees are also coming in the form of out of the ordinary services required by investors.

Schwab and Fidelity also provide their own ETFs, which have underlying fees for the provider. When making a choice of ETFs, the investor needs to compare the fees and consider the historical return with similar ETFs that have the same focus. For example, most providers offer an ETF that is advertised as a mirror of the S&P 500 stock index. Every EFT from the numerous providers will have different fees and slightly different returns even if they mirror the same index.

There is also a difference in the bid and ask of index ETFs. According to Investopedia: "the bid and ask is: The term bid and ask (also known as bid and offer) refers to a two-way price quotation that indicates the best potential price at which a security can be sold and bought at a given point in time. The bid price represents the maximum price that a buyer is willing to pay for a share of stock or other security. The ask price represents the minimum price that a seller is willing to take for that same security. A trade or transaction occurs after the buyer and seller agree on a price for the security which is no higher than the bid and no lower than the ask. The difference between bid and ask prices, or the spread, is a key indicator of the liquidity of the asset. In general, the smaller the spread, the better the liquidity."

For example, the bid ask price of SPY, the widest traded S&P 500 index ETF, is 297.34 and 297.35 while the bid ask price for VOO, an S&P 500 index ETF offered by Vanguard is 273.14 and 273.17. In this random example, an investor would be able to buy the SPY at $297.35 per share and sell it at $297.34. At the same time, an investor would buy the VOO at $273.17 per share and sell at $273.14 per share. This implies a loss of two cents in VOO trades and shows a difference in the two ETFs. For the typical investor, it may not seem like much but can be relevant over time if there are multiple trades.

The zero-commission cost for online trades has the potential to change the industry and not necessarily to the positive. Decreasing costs to the investor is a positive, but if the investor does not know how to best invest for his or her personal best interests, this could be more of a negative. It is apparent that the investor needs to be educated on the process of investing and needs to have a financial plan to use as an overall guide. We keep coming back to the financial plan because it is that important.

Mutual fund purchases online will also be without cost in this new program for TD Ameritrade, Fidelity, and Schwab. If assistance is needed, the fee for the mutual fund trades may be based on the value of the trade or per fund depending on the type of fund considered. Fees for bond purchases and sales are based on the value of the purchase and are an addition to the price of the bond. Many of these companies do not require a minimum deposit, which is a very good way for a new investor to get started in the process.

These companies have trillions of dollars in investors' assets with account sizes from the hundreds to the millions of dollars. While their advertising tout the fees that are no longer being charged, there are still fees for some circumstances. The remaining fees will vary with different account sizes. The higher the balances the client maintains with the provider, the lower the fee structure. These lower fees are negotiated with the firm's representatives. At times the firms offer deals for bringing new money to them such as a bonus to the account balance based on the value of the addition, or other thank-you gifts that may interest the investor.

The tools offered by these companies help the investor understand the nature of investments and many of the basics of managing assets. Asset allocation is stressed, since it is the primary source of return. Various sources and rating services are provided for the investments, particularly stocks, bonds, and ETFs. Many of the advertisements stress the quality, ease of use, and accuracy of these various tools. However, these companies are not fiduciaries. There are subsidiaries that provide fiduciary services but only for the accounts in the high six figures and above.

The typical investor is on his or her own regarding making the primary decision of asset allocation and choice of investment tools to use. The company representative will provide alternatives and will possibly push a specific investment if it is to the company's advantage but will not make the final decision, since the company does not want the liability of the choice.

If the client balance is large enough or if the client provides evidence of more assets elsewhere, the companies may offer individual financial planning services. These services will help the client determine his or her proper asset allocation but will also provide more detail to the service provider of additional assets that may be available for transfer. The provider is not interested in helping clients with debt management and with assets that are not typical investment securities.

When viewing the process from the company's perspective, it is to the company's advantage for the client to make as many trades as possible, not only in buying and selling an asset in reaction to the market but to have numerous assets, as there can be a fee for each transaction, especially if help is needed from a live person. The more securities traded the better. However, if over 90 percent of return is based on asset allocation, the most efficient investor will understand his or her desired asset allocation, make a limited number of trades to accomplish the allocation and then let the market run.

The company would prefer you to study alternatives continuously, make ongoing changes as you convince yourself you could do better, so more fees may be generated. The nature of these investments needs to be stressed and understood prior to investing. Investment companies stress this in their advertisements if you listen to the fast-talking messages at the end of each commercial or in the small print of written literature, but like the acceptance of the concerns and warnings of a public Wi-Fi, very few heed the warning. The investor has been programmed to seek the highest return with the least amount of risk, which is a great philosophy. However, most investors do not understand the inherent risk with investments, particularly equity investments.

It cannot be stressed enough that with increased risk comes the potential for increased returns. Equity investments have had a long and very respectful gain over time. It is difficult to find any investment that has consistently provided such a long-term growth that is as simple to buy into the market. Many investment companies stress these historical gains that have been achieved, and then in very fast sentences and small print, there comes the qualifier of "past results are no guarantee of future results" because of the inherent risk.

Equity markets are volatile, and investing should be with a long-term perspective. Long term implies that to achieve the potential growth that historically has been realized by investors, the asset needs to be held for years, since the growth will not be consistent each year. A stock once purchased may plummet in value for a year but in the following years gain at rates that overcome the initial loss and then double in value. At a different time or other stock, the investment may double in value in the first few months of ownership, followed by substantial losses, and then gains again. Over the long term, however, the stock will probably show a gain.

The investor in equity assets must realize that the initial cash investment may even be lost. Cash that is not expected to be needed for years and will not be a substantial setback if the investment is lost should be a measure as to how much to invest. Most stock investors do not use this filter of potential loss when planning to invest, as the temptation of gain is too enticing. A substantial loss in the market has not occurred since

2008. Even with the loss, the rebound following 2008 was such that the depth and speed of the loss has faded away from investor's minds. The market could have responded in the opposite direction. Due to the nature of equities, a significant loss is possible and will occur at some point. However, the historical record is that stocks recover and move to higher gains over time.

The stock market rally following the presidential election of 2016 came as a surprise to most investors since the winner of the election was a real shock. Prior to the results, the expectation was that the market would crash and burn if Trump was elected and more of the same market conditions as had been experienced if Clinton were the winner. There was no rush to buy prior to the election, but a sense of almost euphoria came over investors after the election of Trump. It was amazing to say the least.

Hardly anyone expected the post-Trump election rally to occur, but it has been a pleasure to experience. Investors need to keep in mind that a market decline of the same magnitude or worse can occur at any time and be just as unexpected as the Trump election rally. If a market decline occurred, many investors would lose money as panic arises with the depth and/or length of the decline and would sell their equity positions. They would sell because they needed the money for other emergency uses. The dollars used in the investment were not in excess but were really money that was parked in the stock market because a quick gain was anticipated. The long-term perspective must be kept in mind during a decline.

In the typical business TV station interview, the host will speak with an "expert" regarding a stock or portion of the market and ask at what price the expert would buy or sell an investment. The expert would provide what seems like very detailed and financially intelligent reasons for buying or not buying and provide prices for entrance into and exit from the investment. The expert does not know how the investment will change, only that given a specific set of numbers and expectations, the investment should perform in a specific way.

However, the expert does not have all the facts. No doubt prior to the election of 2016 that ignited the rally, many experts were making their decisions based on the expectation that Clinton would win. Virtually every forecast for a lower or declining equity investment was completely wrong, and experts making forecasts on today's economy could be just as wrong. Equities are a great investment if the characteristics and expectations are clarified and understood.

This type of discussion hints that the successful investor waits for an opportunity to buy and then can determine when to sell. This is sometimes called "timing the market." Market timing is extremely risky and rarely consistently successful. The long-term perspective that is needed when owning stocks is circumvented when the goal is to instead enter and exit ownership at the most profitable time.

Chapter 9

Traditional Brokerage with Mutual Funds

*The way of a fool is right in his own eyes,
but a wise man listens to advice.*
—*Proverbs 12:15 ESV*

A very common method of obtaining financial advice and thereby a place in the markets is through brokerage services such as Edward Jones, Wells Fargo Advisors, Raymond James, Merrill Lynch, and many others. The full-service brokerage service comes in many forms. One of the more common is the representative in a storefront office in many cities and towns. There are many of these brokers competing for the local business. The representatives usually are from the same town and area they have lived most of their lives. They are local folks who sell investment services, primarily in the form of mutual funds to the local community.

A mutual fund is a basket of securities in which numerous investors are interested in owning this defined collection of assets. There are mutual funds for stocks, bonds, and many combinations thereof that can be used to meet the investment needs of an investor. The number of funds available number in the thousands and are provided by hundreds of companies. Mutual funds are classified by the type of securities in the funds and by three basic types of fee structure of the instrument: front-load, back-load and no-load.

The front-load funds charge a fee to enter the fund. This fee is a one-time charge in the form of a percentage of the purchase. The percentage is usually around 2 to 5 percent of the purchase. For example, if the load is 4 percent, and the investor is placing $10,000 in the fund, the load is $400. If the initial purchase is over $50,000, this load is usually waived.

A back-end load is a fee charged to a mutual fund client if he or she pulls the money out of the investment within a specific period from the initial purchase. For example, a back-load of 5 percent would be charged to the amount withdrawn within a year of the initial purchase. The ending amount withdrawn from a $10,000 investment would be $500, leaving the investor with $9,500. As the length of time from the initial purchase widens, the charge is decreased until after a specific number of years, usually five to seven years, there is no longer a fee for withdrawing.

A no-load fund does not charge a fee to enter the fund or a fee to withdraw from the fund. Like all types of mutual funds, there is always an underlying management fee that is charged to the investor for managing the investment and the accounting necessary to maintain the mutual fund's integrity and obligations to the investor.

The fees are summarized in the prospectus that is provided at the time of the purchase of the fund. The amount of the management fee will vary and should be determined prior to purchasing a mutual fund. Some mutual fund companies share the management fee with the broker selling the fund. This practice can give clients the false impression that their broker is not charging a fee. Any fee that is charged to the investment will decrease the return that is realized. Investors need to be diligent in comparing the various options that are offered.

Many full-service brokers recommend their clients use numerous mutual funds in their portfolio. This practice provides a sense of diversification that usually is good but which can result in a highly inefficient portfolio. These firms usually take their fees from the mutual funds with the various types of compensation. Front-end and back-end loads are used in many of these accounts, and still others prefer to use no-load funds and charge an annual management fee or use mutual funds that pay the broker a portion of the embedded management fee.

Mutual fund managers want their fund to be the best in its class. It is a very competitive business as investors and investment professionals prefer to use those funds that have the best return over time. To become the best or remain as a top fund, the fund manager must constantly look for the best-performing stocks. The individual securities—that is, the specific stocks that are placed in an equity mutual fund—are found by constantly looking at the universe of stocks.

Any stock that is doing extremely well and is providing exceptional returns in relation to others will be evident through research. Fund managers will place the successful stock in their fund to improve the fund's return results. Many other mutual fund managers will place the same stock(s) in their fund because of return. When a client's portfolio has many mutual funds, there is the appearance of diversification, but in fact the actual parts of the funds could be the exact same. The numerous mutual funds will probably provide more protection for the broker than for the client.

If the client prefers to not use mutual funds, the broker may charge a brokerage fee on the purchase or sale of the security. These fees are usually higher than firms like TD Ameritrade or Schwab due to the compensation to the full-service broker.

Brokers are usually in a very competitive market, and the ability to survive the business is difficult. Once hired by a firm, the broker is trained for a year or so. The new hire is compensated with a fixed salary in anticipation of future growth of assets and the expectation that the broker will be successful in bringing in new business.

As the level of assets under the new hire grow, the fixed salary becomes more commission and management fee based. The broker must be comfortable with sales. The initial target of the new hire will be personal family and acquaintances—considered the easiest to gain assets under management. The new hire must also have a willingness to learn the business, to complete the training that results in the necessary licensing, and to regularly hear "no thanks" when speaking with prospects.

The experienced broker's compensation is directly based on the amount of business gathered for the company. More than half of brokers starting the business fail to gather adequate assets to provide the necessary fee income to afford an acceptable compensation for the broker and for the brokerage firm to give support to the broker.

Given this extreme pressure to ramp up an income stream for the broker, the selection of specific assets to recommend to a client will at times lean toward products that carry the highest fees. The products may not be in the best interest of the client. While the specific product may be superior to investments the client previously had, there may be even better products available, usually with a lower fee structure. The broker is in most situations not acting as a fiduciary for the client.

There are also full-service brokers who have been successful and have a respected reputation among their preferred client base. These brokers have many clients who have been with them for many years, even serving multiple generations of the same family. The brokers are considered the experts and have luxurious offices to illustrate their success and to help convince current and future clients of their perceived abilities. After all, a common measure of financial success is often demonstrated in material success and opulence.

These brokers treat their clients very well in the form of gifts, meals, a day at the ballpark, or a special event. The relationship between the client and broker is carefully cultivated by the broker, and maintaining it is extremely important to the broker. The perks that are passed to the client become an expectation and are usually enjoyed by the client since the broker works very hard to understand the client's likes and dislikes. Managing the relationship can become more important than managing the investment to the broker.

Clients that have a long-term relationship with these "generous" brokers are often quite willing to recommend their broker to others. The usual accolades are that the broker is nice, friendly, takes me to the ballgame, treats me to dinners out, does a good job, and calls on a regular basis. The perks received can become the desired result of the relationship in place of consistent long-term growth of investments. The perks enjoyed by clients are not magnanimously provided by the investment company out of its desire to give back but are being spent to keep the client. Most of these clients do not realize how much they are paying in fees and probably do not really care, as the attention and perks received are the valued benefit.

Full-service brokers are also available at banks and credit unions. The broker is often called a dual employee, since the broker has ties to the bank that provides the office, pay structure, and benefits and to the brokerage firm that handles the financial brokerage back office, training, and marketing. Bank or credit union brokers provide the institution the ability to broaden its services to their clients. The fee structure to these brokers is somewhat different than for stand-alone brokers in percentages of commission since the commissions are shared with the bank or credit union.

Securing and maintaining a friendly—and the appearance of a long-lasting—relationship with the client is the primary goal of the broker. It is the appearance of a long-lasting relationship since in reality the friendly relationship will stop as soon as the client moves his or her assets to another provider. Many clients consider their broker as a genuine friend and confidant when in fact it is a service relationship. If the service is no longer being provided, the broker will be much less friendly or generous with time, information, and gifts.

The typical client for the bank or credit union broker is usually a deposit client who is unsatisfied with the low rates and is looking for a greater return.

Chapter 10

The Flexibility of No-Load Mutual Funds

For the Lord gives wisdom; from his mouth come knowledge and understanding.
—Proverbs 2:6 ESV

It is possible to buy a no-load mutual fund by going straight to the mutual fund company. Examples of these companies are Vanguard, Fidelity, and T Rowe Price. There are many more. Most mutual fund companies also offer discount brokerage and other platforms for buying and selling securities. Financial services companies want to be able to offer whatever the investing client is seeking. This provides many choices for the investor but also places an obligation on the investor to understand the various options that are available.

No-load mutual funds provide the ability to buy an investment product at no cost to buy or sell. All mutual funds do have an embedded management fee that can be determined by reviewing the prospectus or/and online summary. Many mutual funds also have different classes of the same fund. The various classes have different levels of management fees due to the intended use of the fund or the purchase size of the investment. For example, if the fund is being used in a retirement fund for a company 401(k), a class of a particular fund would have a lower management fee than the same fund being offered to individual investors.

Most mutual funds have a minimum investment that must be purchased to start the investment. This minimum can be as small as $500 or as large as $1 million or more. The typical is around $2,500 for the average investor. The funds that require a minimum of $1 million will have a lower embedded management fee or may have a special management process that does not want a lot of changes throughout time.

The fund may allow a much lower minimum initial purchase if the investor agrees to make regular monthly payments to purchase more shares at least until the fund reaches the stated minimum. For example, the fund may allow the investor to begin investing with $50 as long as the investor makes monthly payments of $50 or more until the fund reaches a balance of $2,500. This is an excellent way to begin investing but does limit the ability to diversify if the investor has limited cash flow.

There are websites that will provide a rating and methods of comparison for mutual funds. The discount brokers such as TD Ameritrade, Schwab, E*Trade, Vanguard, and Fidelity provide ratings, but an open account is needed to obtain the full scope of the ratings. Yahoo Finance (https://finance.yahoo.com/) and The Street (https://www.thestreet.com/) provide free ratings for various investments including mutual funds. Others are out there.

Morningstar provides very detailed ratings but requires a subscription to use. So is the free service equivalent to the information provided by the subscription? The subscription will provide much more information, but as to relevancy for a typical investor, the subscription would probably be an unnecessary expense.

Chapter 11

RIAs and Bank Wealth Management, a.k.a. Trust Departments: Fiduciary Services Providers

For the protection of wisdom is like the protection of money, and the advantage of knowledge is that wisdom preserves the life of him who has it.
—*Ecclesiastes 7:12 ESV*

The Registered Investment Advisor (RIA) is defined by Investopedia as "a person or firm who advises high-net-worth individuals on investments and manages their portfolios. RIAs have a fiduciary duty to their clients, which means they have a fundamental obligation to provide investment advice that always acts in their clients' best interests."

These service providers are usually looking for the high net worth client and will offer a multitude of services in addition in investment management. Many provide financial planning that encompasses the client's entire estate. The RIA may even have an attorney and or accountant on staff experienced in estate planning and corporate tax law to handle estate planning documents and tax advice to their clients. RIAs provide many services to the high net worth client that are usually not as necessary to the average investor such as family office needs. Since RIAs usually work as a fiduciary, local providers need to be considered when looking for an adviser. Depending on the specific requirements of the firm, it may be a good fit. The overall fee structure needs to be confirmed prior to placing assets with the RIA or for any provider.

Most banks have a department called Wealth Management or in smaller banks may be called a Trust Department. These service providers are fiduciaries. The bank is granted Trust Powers by the banking regulator that the bank is chartered, either state of federal. On a regular basis, the Fiduciary services department is examined by the appropriate government agency to be assured of compliance to applicable laws and regulations.

These departments are operated differently than other service providers. The officers and account managers are usually not on commission and are usually more customer focused than sales centered. Serving as a fiduciary is a primary focus of the administrative officer. A fiduciary services officer, also known as trust officer, is not licensed but must follow strict policies and procedures to meet state and federal laws. He/she is responsible for the management of trusts as outlined in trust agreements and the ongoing investment of assets held by the trusts.

Prospective clients for the fiduciary services provider in banks and trust companies include investors wanting to grow their assets through stocks, ETFs, and other investment instruments like other providers previously outlined. The fiduciary services officer or administrator will also hope to convince clients to name their employer as trustee of their personal trusts and serve in the fiduciary capacities as executor or guardian if the prospect has that need. The fiduciary services officer is expected to understand investments and to correctly follow the terms of a governing document such as a will or trust. Compensation for the fiduciary services officer and administrator is usually salary based with incentives added. The fiduciary standard is stressed, and financial planning is usually a part of the services offered. Coming from the background of a bank trust officer, I see the advantages of using fiduciary service providers in banks and trust companies. Using a fiduciary services provider as an investment manager does give the investor the benefit of enjoying a provider with a duty to place the client's best interest a priority.

The client should still seek to understand the investments being recommended when using a fiduciary as their service provider. Once there is a comfort level with investments, self-directing may be a workable solution, thereby saving the cost of management. The fees used by a fiduciary are usually based on the account balance. A set percentage, from 1 to 2 percent per year, will be charged with a one twelfth of the fee taken each month. A provider who is a fiduciary is worth consideration, especially if the client's knowledge of investments is limited. Knowing that any decision is made with the client's best interest is a distinct advantage.

The bank trust officer answers to a specific committee from the bank's board of the directors, usually called the Investment Committee. The committee could be comprised of members of the board of directors, officers of the bank in other departments such as loan or retail, major stockholders of the bank, or trusted bank clients. Banks have different ideas of who should make up the committee within the guidelines of the regulatory agency. The committee is responsible for the successful management of the accounts in the department and will set various standards, requirements, and needs as outlined by the board of directors and the regulatory agency.

Many providers who are fiduciaries have the training and resources to offer a detailed financial plan for clients. An examination and review of the investor's financial plan is helpful to understand the goals to reach with a knowledge of what products and services will best reach those goals while balancing the risk and fees of the available services.

Chapter 12

Other Types of Investments to Consider

Does not wisdom call? Does not understanding raise her voice?
—*Proverbs 8:1 ESV*

Throughout this book the purchase and sale of common stock has been the focus of needing financial services. The stock may come in the form of individual securities, ETFs, and/or mutual funds. The ownership of publicly traded equity shares of US-based companies has proven to be an excellent way to build wealth over a long period of time.

Many other types of assets can also build wealth that will have very different characteristics and therefore are considered by many investors and financial advisers as worthy of consideration. For example, it is possible to own shares in companies that are based in countries other than the United States. These companies will be subject to the economy and government regulations of their country and will also be subjected to changes in currency volatility between the United States and the country of their base. These differences are becoming less noticeable as many companies have a presence in the United States.

Investments securities are usually categorized as "growth" or "income" in very basic terms. Growth implies the common stock, and income implies securities that are created to produce income as their first priority and growth as a second priority. Examples of income assets are bonds and CDs. There are many types of bonds such as government, corporate, municipal, foreign, convertible, and junk. Depending on the financial plan, the type and quantity of these various types of bonds should be determined. Bonds are also available in mutual funds and ETFs. Bonds are much less volatile than stocks, so while their risk is less than stocks, there is still risk.

Certificates of deposit (CDs) are a very basic form

of investment and have very low risk under most circumstances. With the government FDIC insurance on account values up to $250,000, placing money in a CD is virtually risk free but with a low rate of return. The investor has many choices on where to purchase the CD, and risk and assurance of adequate FDIC coverage should be the primary screens.

Insurance companies offer annuities as a low-risk form of investment. There are many types of annuities issued by many companies. The strength of the annuity is dependent on the strength of the insurance company writing the annuity.

In my opinion, it is difficult to find anything good about annuities. The basic definition of an annuity is that it is a contract between an insurance company and a client. Fixed annuities, the most basic type, can be sold by individuals with an insurance license. The more complicated annuity, such as index and variable, are sold by insurance-licensed brokers. Annuities are known for their high fees, strict rules for distribution and withdrawals, and high commissions to the seller of the instrument.

The income and gains obtained by annuities, if

not distributed to the client, are tax deferred until the funds are received. This characteristic is like an individual retirement account. A typical brokerage account of stocks and bonds generates taxable income in the form of interest and dividends. This income is taxable in the year it is generated, even if the funds are reinvested in the account. This is a benefit for annuity holders in most situations. This advantage does not counter the primary disadvantages of high fees and complicated rules for withdrawal.

Proponents of annuities tout the structure of providing fixed income over a specific number of months or years, but this attribute comes with a very high initial cost in relation to other methods of achieving the same goal with other investments. Whenever an annuity is being suggested as the best alternative for a client, the client needs to get a second opinion, and that opinion needs to come from someone who has nothing to gain from the decision. The second opinion should have the characteristics of a fiduciary.

When the owner of an annuity wants to take money from the account, there are several choices.

The most well-known method is to annuitize the balance. According to Investopedia, "annuitization is the process of converting an annuity investment into a series of periodic income payments. Annuities may be annuitized for a specific period or for the life of the annuitant (the person named to receive the benefit of an annuity). Annuity payments may only be made to the annuitant or to the annuitant and a surviving spouse in a joint life arrangement. Annuitants can arrange for beneficiaries to receive a portion of the annuity balance upon their death."

Since the annuity can be structured to be paid out over the life of the annuitant, there is risk. If the annuitant lives a very long time, that is longer than the expected lifetime, the annuitant may receive more benefit from the annuity than has been paid in or earned by the investment. If the annuitant does not live long after beginning the annuitization, the insurance company has come out ahead. Basically, when an annuity is paid out, the annuitant is betting for a long life and the annuity company is betting on a typical or short life span.

Chapter 13

Alternative Investments

For wisdom will come into your heart, and knowledge will be pleasant to your soul.
—Proverbs 2:20 ESV

With various sources of financial information (not an all-inclusive list) having been briefly described, what is the typical person to do if investments should be purchased? Those described have not always been in the best light, so if a reader has made it this far, I hope there is a lingering question: How do I invest? Managing investments is a learned trait.

We do not hire someone to cook all our meals, wash our clothes, clean our house, mow the yard, or shovel the snow unless we are wealthy enough to have someone do these services for us, or we are unable to do these tasks. We learn how to do these various tasks to save money and have these things done to our satisfaction. There are other tasks, however, such as car repairs, plumbing or electrical concerns, or home repairs that many of us do not feel competent enough to correctly complete these tasks, so a professional or at least someone who knows what to do is found to do it.

It is the same with money management, including investments in the stock market. With a little knowledge and experience, the typical person can take charge of his or her money and manage investments, resulting in substantial savings in fees and a portfolio that meets the individual needs of the investor.

The basic use of percentages and the ability to add, subtract, multiply, and divide are used to create a portfolio. Most financial service providers will make it look more complicated, but it is not. Many services want to use various types of securities and methods that do not necessarily add to the overall growth of the portfolio.

An example of assets frequently recommended but

with sporadic results is a class of investments called alternative investments. An alternative investment is a financial asset that does not fall into one of the conventional investment categories of stocks and bonds. Examples include private equity/venture capital, hedge funds, real property, commodities, and tangible assets.

These investments in theory will go up when the stock market goes down, and in many situations vice versa. In the strong stock market that we are experiencing and have experienced in the recent past, the benefit of these securities is limited. The fees are rather high in comparison to stocks and bonds but do seem to zig when the stock market zags. A concern is that if the stock continues to rise, those dollars placed in alternative investments are lagging, so it is difficult to see the reasoning for their use. Also, in a period of strong pressure to sell stocks, these alternatives do not gain in the ratio as the loss.

Chapter 14

Back to the Heart of It: The Financial Plan

For which of you desiring to build a tower does not first sit down and count the cost, whether he has enough to complete it? Otherwise, when he has laid the foundation and is not able to finish, all who see it begin to mock him, saying, "This man began to build and was not able to finish."
—Luke 14: 28–30 ESV

The key is the financial plan. A comprehensive plan done and explained by a competent and caring individual is a necessity. The plan is a basic yet also full of details like a road map of our financial situation to provide guidance to begin the investment process.

The plan will provide guidance for the asset allocation that is best suited for you. This allocation will provide percentages as to how much of investments should be in stocks and bonds. For example, the plan may recommend 75 percent in equities and 25 percent in fixed-income assets. Specific securities may be recommended to meet this basic allocation, but basically a workable portfolio would be 45 percent SPY, 30 percent QQQ, and 25 percent LQD. The use of three ETFs that are widely traded would meet the asset allocation and provide a low cost and diversification. SPY matches the S & P 500 index, QQQ matches the Nasdaq 100 index, and LQD matches an index of United States corporate bonds.

Other securities could be added, and most financial advisers would probably recommend it, but these three ETFs will provide a very good portfolio. Most of us can manage this basic portfolio. If the account is held with TD Ameritrade, Fidelity, or Schwab offering free brokerage, the investor must determine how much of each security to buy using basic math. If the account is

$10,000, $4,500 is allocated to SPY, $3,000 allocated to QQQ, and $2,500 to LQD. Currently, SPY is around $333 per share, QQQ is $230 per share, and LQD is $130 per share. These three ETFs are some of the most widely traded.

It is never exact, but dividing the allocation by price determines the number of shares. $4,500 divided by $333 is 13.5, so we buy fourteen shares. QQQ will be $3,000 divided by $230, or 13.1, so we buy thirteen shares, and buy nineteen shares of LQD (2,500/130). The account should be set up to automatically reinvest dividends so that the money stays invested. There will always be some cash as the funding cannot be work out to the penny. The account is fully invested at this point. It can be that easy.

A very important task once the account is funded is to rebalance. The percentages of stocks to bonds will change daily as market conditions change. At least annually, the overall asset allocation needs to be reviewed and some securities purchased and others sold to bring the account back into the recommended allocation. Also, on a periodic basis as personal goals and assets change, the financial plan needs to be updated.

This may change the asset allocation, resulting in the change of the securities in the investment account.

If you do not feel comfortable in managing your own investments, then use a service that will allow you to ask multiple questions so you will learn to understand the process. The big discount brokers (TD Ameritrade, Schwab, Fidelity, E*Trade) provide multiple resources to educate on their website. No matter what level of help you employ, having access to one of these providers will answer a lot of questions and in time may provide the confidence to manage your own account. An investment account with a $100,000 balance that is charged a 1 percent fee per year takes $1,000 per year in fees from your pocket. Imagine what you can do with that $1,000 each year if saved!

Chapter 15

Real Risk Tolerance and the Need to Save More

With God are wisdom and might; He has counsel and understanding.
—*Job 12:13 ESV*

Within the financial plan, the asset allocation is the driver to reach the needed return and accomplish the goals that have been outlined. I have mentioned that service providers have easy question-and-answer sheets to provide some insight as to the level of risk that the assets should be placed. These questions include the length of time that the money is available for investment, when the results are needed, how far-reaching the goal is, what experience the investor has with various tools, etc.

These surveys are on the web as well. Some are very involved, and others are extremely simple. The financial plan should have a high-quality method to determine the proper starting point. There is, however, a concern that is not usually addressed in a plan. Suppose your financial plan says you should be aggressive in your asset allocation such that your portfolio is 90 percent stocks and 10 percent in bonds or cash. The decision is based on an extended period of investment in order to reach goals that have been discussed.

However, if you do not like risk—that is, you would be very stressed as you watch the market fluctuate and the market value rise and fall, the calculated asset allocation should be adjusted. The goals should be changed and the funds obtained from sources such as the sale of assets or the need to take on additional work. Alternative resources need to be found to reach the desired goal. Peace of mind is too important, and if your investments are subjected to a greater level of risk than you can personally tolerate, the risk needs to be changed. At this point the asset allocation is settled first, and then a "what-if" financial plan is provided. If the results of this sample plan do not accomplish the necessary goals, then other items must change. The asset allocation is fixed, and other variables are considered.

Generally, most of us have not saved enough to meet future short-term goals and long-term goals such as retirement. It is simply a product of our culture that stresses the present at the expense of the future. Many places of employment used to provide a pension to its employees as an incentive to stay with the company for many years. This was a wonderful benefit of employment and allowed the employee to use his or her monthly income to spend on current expenses.

As interest rates fell over the past several decades, the cost to fund pensions became too much of an expense. While interest rates were falling, the culture became more mobile, and staying with a company throughout the work years became less popular. Also, other benefits such as quality medical insurance and disability insurance became more desirable.

As pensions disappeared, employees were given other tools to save for retirement such as 401(k) plans and individual retirement accounts (IRAs). These plans offered some incentive to save, but the savings became almost solely focused on the employee to take steps to save for his or her own retirement. This savings resulted in a decrease in spending cash that was available on a monthly basis. Most of us chose to keep on spending rather than decrease our available cash to save for retirement.

As a result, our culture is not planning for the future. The sooner each of us determines where we are in relation to where we need to be, the easier the fix will be. It is time to start. I hope this book will help you meet your goals.

About the Author

Will Taylor has more than thirty-five years of experience managing client assets. Raised on a grain and livestock farm in Central Illinois, he worked as a farmer and then a bank trust officer at community banks. He earned a Bachelor of Science from the University of Illinois in Urbana, an MBA from the University of Illinois in Springfield and a certified financial planner designation from the College of Financial Planning. He has worked with many providers of financial services throughout his career. Will and his wife Teri live in Bettendorf, Iowa.